CW01456896

KNOCKING DOWN THE WALL

TREVOR SWISTCHEW

(July 2024)

For Rod Lugg,
Thank you
For Caring,
Your Friend,
Trevor Swistchew.

A NARRATIVE FROM CHILDHOOD

This book is dedicated to my family and to those whose life paths I have crossed and who I may have offended over the years. I apologise to anyone who has encountered my negativity in any way.

May understanding arise in all and everyone realise their duty to protect children throughout the world.

This journal forms chapters of my story arising from years of experience, some of which were lived in children's homes, that impacted my life and consciousness for over 5 decades.

I trust the reader will accept these writings as an effort to inform him or her of the importance of raising children in an open, loving and compassionate way. Any errors in the text are mine as I am writing of events more than 50 years old.

Trevor Swistchew

CONTENT

Part 2_ - KNOCKING DOWN THE WALL

FOREWORD

When I first wrote 'Knocking On The Wall', which was published in 2019, I had no idea of any follow-up story, but recently, having pondered much about the first book (included in this edition as Part One), I have decided to write another, touching and expanding upon many of the themes and recollections of the first book (Part Two) titled 'Knocking Down The Wall'.

Songs that relate to this book can be
found by going to this website:
www.bit.ly/TrevorSoundcloud

The songs are part of my story,
and I hope they will be helpful to you.

INTRODUCTION

All over the world people are protesting about many things. From political corruption to climate change, unfair imprisoning of dissidents and economic inequality, the protests are on the News and Press almost daily. As this continues along, new challenges against authority are everywhere, including protests on working conditions, sea, land and air pollution, the irresponsibility of world corporations, and the privileged lives of the mega rich.

The stark lack of public accountability and questionable oppressive rule in many countries, has inflamed people right across the world and is leading to a street level crusade that has drawn in many individuals from the world of the arts, culture, and sport. With more and more people giving voice to their opposition.

One can only wonder at where it is all going. There is no question that a great deal is unfair and wrong in the world, nor that billions of human beings around the world have no voice or any meaningful choice about their lives or how they are ruled, and this is now expressing itself in protests, peaceful and otherwise and in the most extreme form – as acts of terror.

Humanity is seething on a level never before seen throughout all of human history as more awaken to the lies and untruths and corrupted views that have propagated for centuries. Can anyone in the world justify children dying of hunger in a world where Trillions of Dollars are channelled into the creation of deadly nuclear weapons whose sole reason for their existence is to destroy lives through war? I reject utterly the nonsense that these lethal things are necessary to 'keep the peace.' I start asking, 'whose?'

Has humanity come to a point where people and those who LEAD, are no longer willing to work through their political differences like mature adults? When our attitudes that have developed against refugees fleeing tyranny or injustice or deadly peril at sea, who are then violently repulsed by many European countries for trying to find sanctuary and survive, just ask what exactly has happened to turn human beings into uncaring, unthinking and indifferent people?

It stands to reason that anyone, anywhere in the world, facing oppression or violence would do exactly what millions of refugees are doing right now. They would TRY to protect those they love.

This exposes the hypocrisy and misinformed views proliferating in those among the UK and European populations who hold far-right views, then project unfair discrimination towards displaced men, women, and children attempting to find a country that will welcome them and help them rebuild lives ruined by War or oppression in their own land.

Surely, every human being in the world has the right to exist, and surely everyone has the duty as human beings to help when and where they can. If not, then what does that say regarding our own humanity? When I hear or read hateful views from people online, I feel I have to challenge and question these views because, as a person who questions everything, I feel deeply ashamed that these misinformed views still exist in a world where many people have access to the worldwide network of Communications through the Internet and are certainly more informed and aware of international issues than any previous generation.

I think the world requires an International approach to the way children are schooled and taught so that issues like hatred and mistrust of 'immigrants' can be addressed. This will hopefully lead to a world where hatred and ignorant views are gradually phased out. After all, every person in the world shares the common DNA of everyone else. If THAT were taught to children and young people, the world would, in my view, be happier for it.

PART 1

KNOCKING ON THE WALL

CHAPTER 1

THE WALL

I was born at 3.45pm on August 16th 1950 in the Western General Hospital in Edinburgh, meaning that my star sign is LEO - fiery, direct and outspoken, which has reflected throughout my life in many forms ranging from anger to bluntness and fuelled from a young age by my experience in Childrens Homes from age 6 to 16 ½ years old.

My father was a Russian whose family hailed from St Petersburg and who moved to Poland in the early 1930's for reasons of which I am not fully aware. It may have been the fact that his father had been a Commander in the Red Army and had disagreed with their policy towards countries that were part (albeit involuntarily) of the former Soviet Union. My father, Sergei Leonid Swistchew, came to the UK in 1937 and served on ships in the whaling industry. He met my mother here in Scotland, likely through docking in Leith just after the end of WWII.

They married in 1945/6 and had three children, my brother Stephen, sister Sonia and myself. I heard from an aunt (my mother's sister, Elizabeth) that my father had been challenged for hitting my mother by relatives of the family and apparently had replied that in Russia (at that time), a man who struck his wife was actually showing her he cared and, to him, seemingly, this was the 'norm'. I do not know if this was the fact, but were it so, I could not agree with it. It is never right to assault others, and this may have been one of the reasons they separated when I was around two years old.

Many years later, it was learned that my father had probably gone to America, though it was never actually proven, and no one in the family heard from him again.

My mother, with three small children and no husband, took three part-time jobs in order to feed, clothe, and house us. She cleaned 'Common Stairs' for two shillings per job, she also worked as a waitress in the restaurant of the British Sailors

Society in Constitution Street, Leith, and in Crawford's biscuit factory in Leith.

For a time, she had us living in rented rooms in Leith near Water Street, where her mother, Anne Maguire (from County Kerry in Ireland) and father, Alfred Bloomfield (a Welshman), had moved to after they were married. My mother was always a hard worker, and her sister told her that there was an empty house in Main Street, Newhaven, where she could live with her children. It was essentially squatting since there was no landlord. This changed when Edinburgh Council told her she could stay there if she paid rent since the property was under their administration. She agreed a rent, and we lived there from 1954 to 1958. After that, my family moved to Granton.

.oOo.

In the 1950's/60's living in Newhaven and then Granton in the capital of Scotland, I witnessed many assaults on young children as well as my brother and sister. It was, at the time, accepted as *"how life was"* for parents to hit their children for any transgressions of parental law or rules. It was also commonplace for teachers to hit children with a belt in the classroom, and, at that time, was authorised by the authorities in all regions of the country.

At Ainslie Park school teachers criminally assaulted children almost daily. (Use of the word "criminally" is because children were often hit with unauthorised items.) One of these teachers hit children with T-squares (normally used for drawing lines on the chalkboard) on their rear. He would tell the child to bend over and touch their toes and then hit them with the T=square and shout *"Fore"* as they do in the game of golf.

I also saw teachers throwing tennis balls at children, sometimes hitting them on the face. Another of the teachers would flick your ear with a ruler. All of these assaults would nowadays be reason to sack the teacher from their post.

Any child of the 1950/60's would tell you that they were often told *"Your father will hammer you"* or *"Wait until your Dad gets in"*. Young children being told this would often look very downtrodden knowing that any beating would go unpunished by authority because the police at that time would not interfere in what was regarded as a *"Domestic"*.

That sort of thing was endemic when I was young living in Granton on what was a council estate and I know almost every other child in the area would recall having had the same experience. Authorities ignored what was, in fact, assault or even harm to young children. Fathers and mothers could often be seen belting their children on the street, in shops or even on buses. Most people at the time, saw nothing unusual in that cruelty.

At Ainslie Park school, children were often touched inappropriately by one of the gym teachers as they showered after field sports. On one occasion, a gym teacher was given a beating out of School as he walked to his car. It was in retaliation for touching a boy who had brothers known for being tough and who would not tolerate anything of this sort on their family. He could not go to the Police, or he would have found himself in Court. Street Law?

.oOo.

THE WALL

My brother, sister, and I lived in North Edinburgh with my mother and stepfather. We lived in a three-storey tenement on the top floor of a house where our stepfather was a habitual drinker who was often the worst for drink. He had a low tolerance for children, especially if we made any noise.

My brother, sister and I developed a strategy to avoid his violent temper if any of us made ourselves audible. When we came home after being out and did not want to be hit or shouted at, as was very common, it became our habit to knock on the wall in the stairwell, which was the outer wall of our bedroom.

Any of our siblings who were in the room (where we ALWAYS were when he was at home) would hear the knock and quietly open the front door of the house to allow as silent an entry as possible.

There were times when this did not work, and the result was that you got hammered for the slightest sound.

The violence was continual: slaps on the face and body, often with a leather belt folded in half, and on one very cruel occasion, kicked black and blue, an event that forced me to run away from the house to my mother's cousin's home which was near to where I lived.

I was constantly being told I was a "Russian Illegitimate" person, which was not at all true; my Mother had been legally married to the man who was my father. The reference to Russia was that my father had been born in St Petersburg in Russia and came to this country in 1937 with the intention of joining the Merchant Navy.

My stepfather was a man who, for reasons I have never known, resented Russians.

CHAPTER 2

LAGARIE HOUSE RHU

When I was six years old, my brother Steve, my sister Sonia and I were all put in Lagarie House in Rhu, in late May of 1956. We were driven away from our mother's home, by a male social worker, and placed in front of a very large house in its own grounds. It was over 50 miles away from family or friends or any connection we had to folk who knew the family.

There was no, *"Hello,"* no welcoming smile, and no hug. No awareness of how apprehensive any young child would feel on being put in with other children whom you had never met or seen before in your life.

The matron had no time for upset young children, newly arrived at Lagarie House, most of whom came from poor backgrounds or abusive homes. Most new arrivals were very apprehensive, given that they had recently been (in their view at least) taken against their will to a place they knew nothing about and would not have understood the reasons for being there in the first place.

The Matron would stand the new arrivals in front of all the other children, usually in the Dining Room, which was a large enough area for what really was "public humiliation". My brother, sister and I were called *"The Swistchews from Newhaven"* and would need delousing *"to stop them infecting other children with nits or fleas"* in the home.

My mother had kept us very clean, and that thoughtless and cruel comment is, in fact, not only degrading but a slur on a woman like my mother. She had worked very hard to look after us in extremely difficult circumstances.

I was to learn that all new children, when they arrived, would go through the same routine of being publicly chastised and denigrated showing that systematic abuse was very real in the culture of Lagarie House in Rhu.

At Rhu, a child was not a person, more an object, a unit to be told what to wear, what to say and never to ask questions. This was a lesson not lost on me when I asked Matron where my birthday cake (sent to me by my mother) was, after she had confiscated it on my 7th birthday. I was told it was none of my business.

My sister later saw the remains of the cake in Matron's office and when she told Matron that it was wrong to keep a child's cake she was told to go straight to bed without her evening meal.

On another occasion my sister, who tried to protect me from the Matron who was shouting at me for reasons I do not recall, found herself grabbed and pulled heavily by her hair. She was dragged along a corridor and locked in a cupboard under the stairs all afternoon with no access to even a toilet.

To this day, my brother will not talk about his time there. I know it was not pleasant. He always tried to see the funny side of life; I guess it was how he tried NOT to feel low about being in a home. He did not like Lagarie House and joined the Cubs, which allowed him to get out of the home regularly. On more than one occasion, he ran away and was brought back by the police.

Life in Lagarie House was regimented, but the Home could have been a nicer place except for the cruel Matron. I recall a time when I had a very painful boil on my thumb. When I told the matron about it, she dragged me to her office and cut it off with scissors. It bled all over the office desk, resulting in a string of colourful words from Matron that you can likely guess.

Being only 7 years old, I burst into tears at the pain of what she had just done. My sister heard me crying and burst into the room and was told it was for my own good – no antiseptic – no bandage – just a small plaster - and then ordered to leave the room. My mother was told about the incident by my sister, and later, when my mother mentioned this to the deputy matron, she was told that children in care will tend to *"exaggerate"*.

Again this collusion denied my family the legal right to care and protection within a closed environment.

My recollection of Lagarie House is of a place I have not missed at all in my older life. I was glad to find out it had been closed down. It was a hateful place, and those who knew Lagarie House knew it was unwelcoming and unloving.

In recent years, I have heard of and read the recollections of other men and women who experienced life in Lagarie House. None of these were at all pleasant, but they were most assuredly very similar to the experiences that I had during my time in that awful place. Television programmes have exposed the ugliness of children's homes in all their callousness. It is no excuse to say that it all happened a long time ago.

For those with experience of them, it can feel like it was just last week. The BBC programme about Lagarie House, featuring Mark Daly, was a very poignant reminder to me, and his investigations were an honest picture of how awful that place was.

A few years ago, I tried to get information about my brother, sister, and me being in the children's home in Rhu but could find nothing from The British Sailors Society, which had owned it, except that it had closed. Recently, I found out information from the office of the 'Sailors Society,' as it is now called, and I, along with my brother and sister, received a letter of apology from the Society Headquarters.

I could find no Council in Scotland willing to disclose any information on who had been overseeing the home, and I could find no records to verify that my brother, sister, or I had ever been there.

I was sent an email by a kind worker in an authority in the locality of Rhu proving that my brother, sister and I had attended Rhu Primary School in 1957. We were listed on the Child Attendance records. But for that, my family did not exist nor were there any backing records anywhere in Scotland that I could find in spite of many phone calls and enquiries to various Authorities.

I learned later that all the records on many children had been lost because of a water leakage in a room where they had been stored in England. It was the practice in the 1950s or 1960s to keep files in copy form just to ensure that important information (relating to vulnerable children and their welfare and safety) would NOT be lost. In later years, that information might have been evidence in any legal challenge or proceedings against the Homes or former Staff.

Why was that accepted even years ago?

Children in the 1950/60/70/80's were not regarded highly in those homes that were all over the country, many of them run by religious organisations. It is very shocking that many girls and boys were witness to a culture of outrageous and criminal acts daily as is now emerging from the National Enquiry and other independent investigations. I think even the National Enquiry was overwhelmed by just how widespread child abuse was in these earlier times. Quite frankly, I suggest that if ALL the now adults - who were children in these places - chose to disclose their experiences and the abuse they were subjected to, the reek would rise to heaven.

I have been in touch with the current organisation that runs what is now called the Sailors Society, and as well as the apology to me and my siblings, as I mentioned above, they have assured me that they are doing everything they can to prevent any abuse towards children in future.

CHAPTER 3

PONTON HOUSE

No's 6-8 Magdala Crescent near Haymarket was the street where *Ponton House Lad's Residence* was situated. There was a wooden sign advertising the place to the other residents of the street and anyone who passed by. It was part of an organisation where young *"vulnerable"* lads were placed, like eggs of a type, into a carton. The main office was on the ground floor of this three-storey building on a quiet street next to Haymarket, running towards Corstorphine.

At 14 years old, I was taken there from an aunt's house for Care and Protection. (She was not my real aunt but was a cousin of my mother's, and I called her my aunt.)

I had run away from home due to a severe beating at the hands of my alcoholic stepfather, who liked showing my family who was in control of the house that he shared with my mother, sister, brother, and I. Both my sister and brother had run away from the dreadful atmosphere before. My own running away wasn't far behind.

Try getting told you are a *"Russian (illegitimate person)"* on many occasions followed by a good kicking and you will soon realise why, after a particularly brutal beating, I took off wearing only a pair of jeans, no socks or shoes and arriving at my *"Aunt's"* house crying in pain.

She cleaned me up, washing the dirt off my feet and skin, appalled at the bruising on my back from the beating I had suffered. I was told that I could stay with her and her family. I wasn't going back to that man, and she gave me a shirt and jumper belonging to one of her 12 children. Her husband and two brothers left the house that night to *"hunt that man"*.

They didn't find him that night — if they had he would have been hurt very badly. I knew that from the look on their faces when they saw how bruised I was and when they asked how I had been hurt.

I stayed with my aunt for a while until one day a man turned up from the Council with a "Care and Protection Order" turning me over to Ponton House Lad's *Residence*. It was frightening going with him to an unknown place.

I didn't know then what was happening but found out later that my aunt had contacted the Council because she had such a large family of her own and could not cope with another mouth to feed. She could not send me back home because my mother and step-father had left Edinburgh and she did not know where they had gone. I was put into a car, driven to Ponton House Head Office at Tollcross, and then taken to Ponton House Lads Residence

I was met by the Superintendent and his Deputy and taken into their office. The door was locked, and I was invited to sit on the deputy's knee. Were they showing kindness to a confused, upset young lad? How could a 14-year-old know the intentions of grown men who were authority figures?

To illustrate the context of this, one only has to think of the same thing happening now, with a National Inquiry in the process of gathering information on predators of young children, to see the fault in what an Officer in a lad's residence had asked of me.

Desperate for some kindness and compassion I naively did as he asked and instantly felt his hand inside my trousers. I immediately pushed him away, stood up and shouted very loudly, I might even have sworn - I know I was angry – I know I was upset – I know the superintendent opened the door very quickly and told me it was just a joke. "*Go along boy, it is alright*".

I ran into the games/television room where other lads were playing snooker and watching television. I tried to tell them what I had just seen and felt. One of the lads said that the Superintendent and Deputy always saw new boys on their own. Other lads said they knew about it and that money or sweets were given to lads that went along with it or who went to "parties" and were given alcohol. If that is not grooming I don't know what is.

I don't recall exactly how long I was at Ponton House. I do know that the police were there one day when I came back from school. The superintendent and his deputy were taken away by the police and I learned later that they were both jailed.

I remember Ponton House being closed and I was taken with two other boys to Wellington Farm School - again for *Care and Protection*. How empty these words are when you think of what children experienced at the hands of adult men and women who were these guardians of child welfare.

CHAPTER 4

WELLINGTON FARM

What exactly are Human Rights? I can tell you what they are NOT. Human rights are supposed to apply to people of all ages and even to the unborn child.

When a person is born, they automatically have the right to life—that is to say they are entitled to such Care and Protection as may be required for their survival. Those charged with this "Duty of Care" MUST deliver it to the best of their professional skill and MUST NOT wilfully neglect or forgo any aspect of the newly born person's wellness.

When children are young, they begin to accumulate the skills, ideals and attitudes that will shape their lives, and it is when very young that a child is most vulnerable; therefore, HOW they are managed in the care of parents or authorities is of the greatest importance. Not only for food, shelter and basic needs, but also the happiness and outlook of the child formulates at this time, and so it is very important that children are raised in a loving, caring and non-threatening environment.

If this process is disrupted, the effects can greatly harm the child, and, unfortunately, many of the world's children already know this, even if they cannot articulate or explain it to others. One only has to look into the eyes of a child to see happiness or sadness instantly, and it is the duty of all people to at least raise their children as well as they can, and to protect them from harm.

Most parents and children's workers want only the best for their children in the 21st century and there are laws in place to protect children in Scotland but, just 5 decades ago, they were abused in their thousands in Children's Homes and Approved Schools. I know this from direct experiences in my youth, when I spent time living "in care".

From beatings to verbal and sexual abuse incidents, I know my own life has been impacted in ways that would fill many volumes were I to try to write it all onto paper. I can recall some very specific "*abuses*" from those in authority, not least the forcible removal of my liberty and being treated like a criminal at Wellington Farm School near Penicuik. I was incarcerated there for 1 year and 3 months, alongside bullies, *"hard men,"* and often uninterested staff who really saw me as just another felon – although I had not been sent there by any Criminal Court, but by a Care and Protection Order signed by a County Court judge.

Once in the system, all human freedom is revoked and the process of depersonalising you starts. They de-louse you, take all your clothes, and any personal property, cut your hair into their style and put you into a uniform. Then they would send you to one of five "Houses" which divided boys into groups led by a House Captain.

Wellington Farm housed more than 90 young boys from ages 14-16. They were from working class families in Glasgow, Edinburgh, Fife and elsewhere. A few of them belonged in the Care And Protection group and the other boys had arrived from Court for criminal acts like theft or assault or entering premises intending to purloin other folks goods. You could say they were minor offences, yet the law is law and thus young folk could be put into an Approved School usually located in the country away from cities and passers-by.

You quickly learn the Unofficial Rules enforced by the House Captain and his lackeys (guys who do the punching and kicking and enjoy the status of being in the Quasi-Elite clique) whose fists, heads and boots are used wherever required to assert the House Captain's authority (mostly a dictator type regime) over all the lesser ranking boys. The only way out was to be as tough as or tougher than the lackeys. That was not me, a quiet, very shy wee laddie who was never a fighter – just another lost boy in a faceless and sometimes quite heartless excuse for a School allegedly *"Making men from boys"*.

I recall one day asking another boy at the school when visits were allowed and getting told that visits could be stopped any time the Headmaster thought so. Just think about that for a minute – you are taken to a place you know NOTHING about, everyone is a stranger, and you are greeted NOT with a welcoming smile but a command to march into the Headmaster's office, stand still, keep quiet and listen!

Then you are in a room with three male staff who tell you to strip off. You awkwardly remove your clothes and go into the shower room where other naked boys are already getting dressed in their House uniforms. There are no curtains or doors on the showers, therefore you try to get washed as privately as you can, all the while being watched by the staff. You are just 14 and you are apprehensive to say the least, not that anyone seems to care. You emerge from the shower, are thrown a towel and told to be as quick as you can. Some introduction into the place you were forced into for *Care and Protection*!

From there you are marched to lunch in the school dining room (*left, right, left, right, shoulders back laddie*) and you enter to a very noisy crowd of boys sitting at their House tables (d*ivide and rule?*). You collect your meal and sit on the last seat on the table which identifies you as the newest *pupil* and endure the barrage of questions from the hard-core.

"What are you in for?"

You stupidly blurt out, "Care and Protection."

Only to hear the reply to the loud sneers and laughter of your compatriots, "So you didnae get caught by the polis then?"

"No. I came from a lad's residence where the Superintendent and his Deputy were both arrested and imprisoned for offences against children and the Court decided that I was requiring *Care and Protection*."

In the days that followed you had to learn a lot of things –

No. 1: Try not to offend anyone.

Some of the boys will want to fight you, sometimes just for looking at them. In your own mind you are actually just curious, a stranger in a strange land and you are trying somehow to create a link, a bridge to other people because you are aware that you HAVE NO CHOICE but to make friends to watch your back from rival boys in other Houses, who were already streetwise enough to compete as their survival instincts (and beatings) had taught them.

No. 2: Don't lose your House merit points.

Merit points were *"awarded"* by staff for a House being clean and passing the daily inspection run by the (ex-military) Headmaster. Every boy was given a job by the House Captain and if it won the House points, that boy was rewarded, or if it lost, the boy responsible was punished by the House rules. (The House Captain oversaw the "rules"). The rules were NOT List D School regulations – they were the Captain's rules, and he could reward or punish any boy he chose. Staff all knew about the *underground* rules but seemed to leave it to the five House Captains to keep their own Houses in compliance. This would suggest that staff were complicit in hundreds of assaults on young boys.

Rewards could be that an individual boy would be excused "latrine duty" for five days (ie he would not have to clean the dormitory latrine). That was a bonus to any boy because any dirt found in the toilet by the Headmaster at the daily inspection could cost ten House points and that poor soul would be sent "round the dorm". Going round the dorm meant that you were sent to each boy's bed after lights out and he had to punch you on the jaw. There were 28 boys in a dormitory which meant that you were punched 27 times – furthermore if you cried you were sent for another round. (I went round the dorm a few times for not cleaning a mirror well enough and on another occasion for trying to inform staff of the brutality of that rotten place).

Another very cruel Captain's rule was the one that forced boys who did not punch you hard enough on the jaw, to follow you in turn and be punched as well. It was ironic that YOU had to punch a boy who might have tried NOT to punch you too hard.

To this day I have crooked teeth in my lower jaw as a result of this.

Few boys challenged the House captains and I was involved more than once in fights due more to my not really having enough street savvy to sense. For example when I was offending a person from another House by something I said or how I looked at them. It was a time of trying to learn to walk on rice paper without tearing it!

In "Wellie" Farm as it was nicknamed, all boys were sent to bed at 9pm. A male staff member would come into each dormitory and yell "Last Call for

Premises". This was to inform the boys that if they needed to use the toilet they had to do so before it was locked for the night. Fail to go and you could wet your bed (or worse) and then the House Captain could send you on the nightly journey round the dorm to receive your punishment. If you had wet the bed , it was found out during the daily inspection by the headmaster, who would deduct house points, thereby invoking the "round the dorm" punishment. Think of the inhumanity and cruelty of denying access to a toilet to more than 28 boys overnight. It served no purpose other than to remind you that someone higher up decided when you could heed the call of nature.

If there are people in Scotland who flaunt the law, is it any wonder when you stop to think of how many of them were "regimented" this way in their early years? Why would adults be any different when they have similar experiences?

At mealtimes, which never varied, the boys all had to get in step and march from work or recreation, or wherever they were, to the dining room. The menus were written for the week, and there was no choice.

Friday was mince pie day with beans—a real delicacy that young lads saw as a high point in their humdrum lives.

At the time of my residency at "Wellie" Farm, my mother was living in England, so I got no visits except for my sister (my brother was always on ships and not in Scotland a lot). I recall a few happy times when I was allowed to go to her house (she was married) for an overnight stay. I was allowed to wear my own clothes for the first time in months, and I went on a bus to her house feeling like an ordinary person. Watching television and making a cup of tea was really great, and I saw the joy in putting on the kettle and making tea as part of the series of little things that gave life its sense of continuity. (The Authorities, in taking these small things away from men or women who are in prison or List D schools, actually add to the suffering of anyone who is placed in their hands.) As I unmask all these ploys and means, I see them now as a definite strategy to control people and undervalue them as human beings, and if that sounds dramatic, it damn well was.

Looking back on my time at Wellington Farm, I can say that I should never have been sent there. It engendered in me a deep sense of distrust and disgust at the apathy of Care and Protection Orders and the men and women who carry them out, and it added only suffering to my life.

Did it grant some wisdom? I leave it to you who read this to think about it.

I learned that heavy-handed rules and invisible regulations do NOT make men out of boys. What they do achieve is to load unnecessary suffering onto people that often causes them to project unwarranted anger and blame onto innocent bystanders.

It has to be asked why the Law at that time allowed children who were put into places like Wellington Farm on Care and Protection Orders no real freedom? After all, they were NOT criminals. I assume the local authority was fully aware of this and their own hand in it, seeing that they did NOTHING to stop it from happening to many young boys and girls. It would have been easy enough to allow a little freedom to non-convicted children to allow them to feel less oppressed, yet it might have been that the Home Office judged everyone as equal in the injustice known as APPROVED SCHOOLS.

I returned to Wellington Farm years later and spoke to the then Headmaster, who denied that anything untoward had ever happened there. I had to point out a great many instances of this to the man. It was very apparent that he either knew nothing or he was saying nothing. I also tried to obtain data relating to my time there from the local authority, which was sent from Midlothian Council to Borders Council, each passing the buck to the other. I was told that there were no records regarding Wellington Farm with either council. Where are they?

I want answers to the questions I am asking in this work.

I also want to know what logic decided that it was all right for the Authorities to dump children into places which were NOT appropriate for that person's human needs.

CHAPTER 5

AFTER WELLINGTON FARM

I was 16 years old when I left Wellington Farm School, a place where I learned to completely mistrust those in authority. I knew that the Care System was rooted in hypocrisy and control.

I was taken to a halfway house in Leamington Terrace near the King's Theatre in Edinburgh. The superintendent helped me to find a job at a timber firm where I worked as an apprentice sawyer. I was only in that job for a few months, leaving after I was approached by another employee who perhaps saw my vulnerability and made my life unbearable by improper suggestions and innuendos. Over the next 25 years I had a total of more than 20 jobs. The childhood issues I experienced meant that my whole life has been coloured with a deep hatred of authority and the feeling that anyone who exercised any power over me could not be trusted.

Thereafter I stayed with my sister, who was now married with a child, in Leith and then Muirhouse Green but she was busy with her family. I drifted into being involved in drugs and religion and played at being a hippy for a couple of years.

In the early 1970s, I lived in a squat in London and learned how to play guitar. I returned to Scotland and became a busker on Rose Street while living in an ashram (hippy commune). At the time, I regarded them as the family I was so desperate for, but I now realise that they, too, were escaping from reality through drugs and drink. However, I became interested in Buddhism and found that this philosophy helped me cope with life.

After six years, I decided that it was time for me to do something with my life, and I enrolled in Moray House to study for a diploma in community work. I lasted for ten months of the course before I was expelled because I constantly questioned and argued with my tutor about his teaching. He was actually correct in throwing me off the course. I was far too argumentative and aggressive to be of any use to anyone who required those in authority to get them a house or help with benefits. When you don't trust authority, you will see indifference even when it does not exist.

Years later, I gained an HND Diploma in Communication, largely due to the help and encouragement of my ex-wife. I met her at Moray House, and we eventually married and even bought a house, but I found it impossible to settle down and become the kind of partner she wanted and deserved.

Although I had left drugs and alternative living behind, I was still drifting from job to job and being aggressive with anyone in authority. This eventually led to us divorcing which may have been the shock I needed. At the age of 56, I had a retail job that lasted for six years (which was a record in my life). I then joined another organisation, based nearer to the flat I had moved into after my divorce, and worked there for seven years until I retired.

I am keen on gardening, writing songs, stories and poetry. I sing and record original songs with people I do trust, those who don't act superior or try to manipulate or use me. They are friends with no official or personal axe to grind and it is for those kind of friends that I am grateful. I also campaign online and on national radio for FAIR PLAY IN ALL LANDS. I no longer believe in most of the things that I had been conditioned to believe when I was a younger person. I think the only intelligent way to live your life is to think for yourself and think BEFORE you accept anything as true or valid in your life.

I have known many other people who were in care and they all tell the same tale of alienation, abuse, not being listened to, living with shame, mistrust and NOT achieving a sense of satisfaction from life. Family estrangement, divorce and often no communication with their own children are also included in personal fallout.

Everyone fails at times, but abused people are so much more obstructed because their past experiences often get in the way, not allowing the individual to see clearly or get past barriers.

CHAPTER 6

CONCLUSIONS

The truth is simply this; if you were abused as a child, your life is permanently tainted and that has to be acknowledged, worked through and understood before you can really move forward and try to find a way to make the most of your remaining years. How many people are alive today who have chosen to bury their past or deny it, living lives dominated by guilt or shame for events that they were NOT responsible for?

"Knocking on the Wall" was written for them as well as for myself. It could have contained a lot of graphic detail about things I experienced and it could have shown all the ugliness and cruelty of abuse.

I chose instead to try to catalogue what I had lived and still live with and try to encourage anyone with this kind of experience to facilitate their own release to some degree from the memories stemming from childhood abuse in writing, or on record.

If any reader has experience of, or knows any child at risk of, abuse there are organisations who can help. Most of them are linked to other specialised agencies and will offer support and guidance to anyone coming forward. (A list of Agencies can be found at the end of the book.)

I hope a time will come when children do not have to live with abuse and that it will be something that will never occur. (Realistically that might never happen but even to ensure that opportunities to abuse children in care are minimalised is surely a start). It is vital to expose abuse wherever and whenever it occurs and surely all adults have a duty to protect children from those who would prey on them.

.oOo.

When a young person is unfairly or cruelly treated in Care he or she will carry their memories with them for life. That is true for all who were abused in Care.

It has to be realised that the effects on those who were abused are many. There is not just the physical pain of being assaulted nor the humiliating suffering that arises from any sort of sexual abuse; there is also the guilt and sense of shame and lowered self-esteem that is permanently stamped upon the young person's consciousness. In later life, this will lead to feelings of anger, inadequacy, and lowered ability to fully participate in life or opportunity, which in turn results in lack of achievement and in some people it can lead to self-harm.

There are people who were abused when they were young who DO achieve their goals, but for many, success always seems beyond their grasp, and this has a direct effect on their attitude towards life. Those who work in childcare or counselling can explain how this process unfolds far more clearly than I can, but even the most superficial investigation into the positive or negative effects of child abuse will prove the validity of these words. It may even provide one with an insight into the myriad of issues that arise from how one is raised.

I can see now how my own life was shaped and distorted by my experiences and the obvious lack of compassion or genuine concern at the hands of some of the people who had authority over me when I was young within the Care system.

Was it that they were poorly trained? Or was it that many of those who worked with children followed the idea that children should be seen and not heard?

I would also like to point out that in instances where abuse was reported to staff, it appeared nothing was done to stop abuse or take ownership of the complaint. This means that in the era of which I speak, there was no accountability or transparency in the way children were looked after, which is why my brother, sister and I were not looked after fairly. How a child is raised impacts the whole of that person's later life. I know from experience that how I view the world and myself is shaped by previous events.

I now realise that in my earlier adult life I deeply resented any show of authority from those who were senior in rank to me. I have had more than 40 jobs in total during my life, some of which I walked out of when managers or owners talked down to me. I was talked to like that in the Children's Homes and I was NOT putting up with that from a boss.

Readers will know that when a person changes jobs far more than usual, it is logical that earnings will be affected to the disadvantage of the person concerned. My life would certainly have been more secure had it not been tainted by my experience of *Care*.

.oOo.

What is it about power that often results in the abuse of one person or persons by someone in authority? Is it just that the authority figure is a bully who enjoys and indulges in intimidating or humiliating other people? Is it simply that they have the desire to "control" others? Or is it that power corrupts and subverts any human feeling that the person has?

No person in the world is unaffected by their own life experience and if you want to figure out why abuse occurs, you have to deconstruct the life experience of the abuser. Cruelty experienced when young weaves itself into your life, shaping and influencing how you think about and view the world, yourself and other people. Therefore, how you relate and think about other people will be linked to your own experience.

My brother, sister and I all know from experience that cruelty and emotional bullying creates suffering and that it is inexcusable when cruelty is meted out in the Care System as it was in the Homes which they and I experienced.

CHAPTER 7
WHY REDRESS?

The reason why redress is required for time in 'Homes' where children suffered abuse is not easy to explain to anyone who has no direct experience. However, any debate on this delicate issue must be aware of the lifetime effect on the individual who lived it (for any length of time). Anyone who suffered abuse in a Home has painful memories of their experience, even if that person cannot relate how or what they feel to other people.

Many who have had this experience of abuse in their childhood often try to forget and ignore their past. That does not undo the abuse, nor does taking intoxicants to forget, which can often result in drug dependency or alcoholism. The fact is that the individual will carry the suffering for the rest of their life. Emotional, physical or sexual abuse are all violent actions towards the child, whose mind cannot and does not understand why they are being hurt or intimidated or manipulated by a "grown-up" – all they know at that time is that something bad is going on and years of guilt, anger and frustration follow on from that.

Low self-esteem and lack of achieving their full potential is a reality for many who were abused in their youth.

That is not to say that those who were abused in Children's Homes must always fail (and there are always those who will aspire and achieve, despite their pain or experience) but it is very much harder for abused children to advance in life, given that all of them feel hindered by memories and pain that they cannot forget.

It is not just the emotional damage that has to be a factor in arriving at what might be seen to be "fair redress". It must also incorporate cognition of the economic loss to the person and how it affected them and their families. Many people are not able to work at all, having drug, alcohol and many psychological problems as a legacy from their time of being in "Care".

In retrospect, I now know that the experiences I had within Children's Homes, which lasted more than 10 years in total, reduced my ability to apply myself to my work in whatever job I was in and thus reduced my earning power and progress in a career path which would have allowed me to achieve sustainable and ongoing prosperity.

In finding and keeping a job, a person has to be motivated and confident of their own abilities, and they must also have a rapport with their employer and colleagues, as anyone will agree. For those with painful and hurtful memories of abuse, the road is littered with their suffering and anger within their own mind.

The combination of these elements is a barrier to open communication and means that the individual does not and cannot conform to the degree of compliance which advancement and achievement demand in the workplace, resulting in a lifetime of low wages, non-fulfilment of potential and limited economic life. It is extremely difficult to convey how that impacts how one feels knowing that one cannot engage fully or actively in these activities, which most people consider normal.

For example, going on holiday, buying new clothes, socialising with friends, and purchasing things one would like to own are all things that millions of people around the world do. It feels as if Oliver Twist is looking through the window at all the wealthy people feeding at an overloaded table.

It also can get you dismissed or cause you to leave a job if the atmosphere is threatening in any way. People who have had no abuse in their lives are much more able to progress in a career. It is not the same for those who carry the residual hurt and guilt of abuse.

CHAPTER 8
CULTS AND CONMEN

In trying to assess the impact of child experiences in care, it is necessary to look at one's past life from the years in which abuse happened through one's teenage years into adult life and into one's present age.

Not only did my working life (and therefore earning power) suffer, so too did I, having to try to relate to other folk in the world, including close family and friends. I know that some of the paths I took were harmful and had a negative impact on me, in so far as my whole life outlook was tainted to the point of being distrustful towards everyone, even those I had grown up with or shared accommodation with.

I was involved with drugs, quasi-religion and even a cult. I was a vulnerable young lad who was looking for acceptance, which I now see was what led me into the associations I had with people and organisations wherein another kind of abuse was rife. That of coercion, manipulation and wilful exploitation of participants.

People in religious cults worked for no wage or any employers liabilities, thinking (having been told) that the work they did was "service to God, the world or the organisation".

Had I NOT come from a life of abuse in care, it is fair to say I may not have been so easily misled or conditioned by people or organisations into following a cult for nearly five years. I was very conditioned when involved in the cult, to the point where the *Truth* they taught was ABSOLUTE to my way of thinking.

I now see, years later, that some teachers are not worthy of trust and that many young, vulnerable people are targeted by followers and groomed into joining. I have had first-hand experience of this and have known a few people who, like myself, have left religious organisations, quite rightly, because of how they were conned into joining at a point in their lives, usually when what they were actually looking for were friends and acceptance in a world which had treated them badly.

Drug abuse is another area in life wherein naive, vulnerable people are pulled into the murky underbelly of towns or cities where the dealer is using their naivety to sell and make a profit from drugs. The usual ploy is to sell young folk the idea that taking drugs is *cool* and that the drugs will show them the truth about life. Old hippies used to have a saying, "Tune in, turn on, drop out," to the pulsating beat of drug music popularised by certain rock bands who could well afford the rehab, which was denied by most working-class users.

I do NOT recommend taking drugs as any honest path to gaining genuine insight, and I know the impact of abusing drugs. The pain of imagining that you know something that other people don't while, in reality, you are deluding yourself.

The all-night deep discussions in squalid candle-lit pads with other stoned people, the lack of sleep, the lack of a decent wash, and the process of thinking you are somehow revolutionary because you don't conform. The zeal with which you try to convince or convert others to what you believe or think. The smug sense of superiority towards all the "squares" who live their illusionary lives of work, taxes, and the Church. All of this springs from your own previous life of experiencing abuse in children's homes, where you learned that your own life had no value to those into whose care you were put, without any rights or say in the matter. Later, as one learns more about self, it dawns that years were wasted following ideas that no-one understood. Moreover, one thought it right to try to convert other folk, even family, to those ideas which had little meaning to those who had not been groomed by the cult or its followers who were idealists yet also naïve about how to change the world, running around with a handful of dreams and the immature wish to get all the other people on side.

For what?

I now realise I was doing that because I naively thought that the more who were part of the Revolution, the faster the world would change into my fanciful ideal.

It was false, and so was I. I left after a few years and I never went back. It was another diversion, another brick in the wall that I had created around my life to keep other folk and their influence out.

CHAPTER 9

RECOMMENDATIONS

I thought it would be useful to think of ways to prevent child abuse in care and put them onto paper as you will read in the list that follows. Had these been in place when I was a child I might have avoided a lot of pain.

Children could wear a security bracelet on their wrist with a signal that informs Local Police at times of danger.

All Homes should have red notices and Freefone numbers where staff, families and children can report abuse.

All staff working with children would be informed that abuse always leads to prison time.

Staff are legally obliged to disclose or whistle blow on any abuse witnessed (enforced by law).

All Homes would have a hotline which is directly connected to the Police.

RECOMMENDATIONS

Offending Children's Homes should be heavily fined and held to account for any abuse, no matter which staff are involved (this would force much stricter recruiting).

Spot inspections on a regular basis.

In-house cameras in ALL Homes.

All staff photographed and displayed in the Homes.

Children taught how to report abuse.

CHAPTER 10
STATEMENT TO THE NATIONAL CONFIDENTIAL FORUM

Date June 8th 2016

The following statement was written by myself as an attempt to convey the lifelong impact that abuse has had on my life. It was submitted to Celsis as an outline and brief explanation of said abuse on my life. It is not an exhaustive statement and therefore is only included in this book as testimony and hopefully inspiration to others who may have suffered abuse to disclose their own story.

This is an attempt to inform readers of the long term effects of abuse when young.

When children are raised in an overly hostile, invasive way they grow to be adults with no trust, or faith, in figures of authority. That is simply the fact of the matter.

The experience I well recall from knowing what it is to be "in care" is an experience of brutality and indifference shown by those who were trusted to carry out their duties and functions towards vulnerable young people. I can quote many instances of how I grew to be the person I am today stemming from personal experience of over 50 years ago when I was young, coming from a home where cruelty and violence were meted out almost daily by an alcoholic step-father, to my "imprisonment" in Children's Homes and a List D (or Approved) school.

My mother and step-father left Edinburgh when I was 14 leaving me to live with a family friend. She had a large family of her own and could not cope with another mouth to feed therefore she contacted social services. They placed me in a children's home but when it closed following the arrest and conviction of the Superintendent and the Deputy who oversaw the Lads Residence, as it was called, I was then placed in an approved school for my own *Care and Protection*.

The emphasis in "care" ought to have been on helping the young grow into positive ways of living—

at least that might have been the original intention. The reality was very much on making it known that those in authority were in charge, with power to reward or punish as they saw fit. Many men and women with direct experience of this will know of what I speak. At 73 years of age, my life is still affected by childhood experiences.

I resent **ALL** forms of authority. I do **NOT** trust those who either have or seek power over others, and I am angry that rhetorical analysis does not openly admit either guilt or shame.

A person is the result of their upbringing, and their earning power is definitely lowered by negative experiences when in their "formative" years. I know this from experience, and my work record shows my exit from any job that I saw as overbearing. In the world, any person's earning power depends on a number of factors – including the ability/skill to perform a role in the workplace; a positive outlook, along with the emotional balance to learn/listen/evolve; and Focus, drive, and a sense of belief/faith/trust in one's boss/manager. All of these things are affected if one has low esteem for self or mistrust of others.

I have had more than the usual number of jobs during my "working life," some lasting only days or longer depending upon how I related to those in superior roles. I can give instances to any who inquire.

From experience, I know that heavy-handedness results in conflict within the person affected, who will generally grow to mistrust even well-meaning people.

I purport that the abused can, and do, often become the abuser.

In any common-sense view, those who study abuse often find a pattern of abuse toward that person when young.

If children are to be protected in care now and in future, they **MUST** have the certainty that they will be listened to.

.oOo.

In making this statement, I have tried to be as accurate as possible. However, some details are sketchy, resulting from the fact that these events took place over 50 years ago. Also, I have found that in trying to secure responsibility for the overseeing of the establishments named, information has not been forthcoming from those I have approached. Therefore, in offering this information, I can only say that any inaccuracies are caused by the above factors.

From 1956-1965, at different periods in that decade I was resident in 3 council administered children's or young persons residences. These were:

Lagarie House Children's Home at Rhu Dumbartonshire (owned at that time by the British Sailors Society). I was there approximately 6 months in 1957 along with my brother and sister. We were placed there to give my mother respite from being a mother with 3 children whose husband had abandoned her and us. The Home was run by a matron whose method of looking after children was that they should be seen and not heard. Tough discipline was her way of letting children know she was in charge and my time there as I recall was quite oppressive and unhappy. Two instances of her methods are as follows – on one occasion I had a boil on my thumb which was full of green coloured fluid. When I told her of this she took me to her office, took a very sharp pair of scissors from her drawer and proceeded to lance the boil. No antiseptic was used and I was given a row for crying. I was 6 years old. In another instance my mother had sent me a cake for my 7th birthday which was subsequently taken away from me, my brother and sister and used for staff tea break. The general atmosphere in that place was one where children residing there were very aware of how they would be dealt with if they crossed any lines, and, in fact, my sister was locked in a cupboard one day for 4 hours in the pitch dark with no water, she still recalls that to this day and she is now nearly 70.

My stepfather was an alcoholic, an ex-navy man and a strict disciplinarian. He came into my family's life in 1958. To look at, he was a smartly dressed, articulate man and, at that time, a Freemason in Scotland. However, drinking brought out what could only be called his alter ego, and as our biological father was

Russian, my stepfather became racially abusive towards us and, on one occasion, came close to very seriously injuring my brother. My brother actually threatened him with a gun after one particularly cruel incident. The atmosphere could be very hostile when he was drunk, and in 1963, he beat me so badly that I fled the house half-naked. My "aunt", who lived nearby, took me in and refused to let me return to my own house because of the injuries to my back in particular, leading to back problems that trouble me to this day. Shortly after I went to stay with my "aunt" my mother and stepfather left Edinburgh to live in Corby, Northamptonshire, leaving me at age 14 with my "aunt's" family. She had 14 children of her own and could not manage to look after me as well, and I was referred by the social work department to go to **Ponton House (Lads Residence),** Edinburgh, for my care and protection since I was still a minor. The people in charge preyed upon the vulnerability of the young children put into their care at that time, and approximately two to three months after I took up residence at Pontin House, the superintendent and deputy were imprisoned on child abuse charges. I was then placed in a List D (Approved) school, **Wellington Farm School,** for my care and protection. The majority of residents there had broken the law in some way or another, and as such, I was a target, being a young, vulnerable, timid boy at that time who found the harsh reality of being denied any freedom or liberty extremely upsetting. My questions to the staff on why I was there were always met with the same reply, "You are here to be looked after until you reach the age of 16."

Violence and beatings from other boys and the quite alarming indifference from some of the staff towards the young residents emerging for breakfast with black eyes, very bad bruising on their faces and other marks of violence on their persons taught me that whenever people have authority over the weak, they will tend to abuse it. I could elaborate on some of the horrors I witnessed in Wellington Farm, which literally made boys wet themselves with fear. I was a resident at Wellington Farm for one year and three months when I was released to a halfway house in Leamington Terrace in Edinburgh. My time there was certainly an improvement over the previous year and three months. The family who ran the halfway house were kind, decent people, and after I left there, I tried to get my life together as best I could.

It is extremely painful to dredge up memories of things you would really rather forget, but I know at my age now the long-term effects of what I suffered when I was a young person. I could have given many, many more examples of the mistrust I have experienced, the anger, the frustration, the pain of feeling the things I have felt, getting divorced from my wife, and losing contact with my family, which I feel all started with the experience of being in care and protection.

If you feel you would like to ask further questions, you may do so. This statement is not exhaustive, nor can it articulate the feelings of pain left from the experiences I went through.

It is presented in the hope that this information will help other children not to be abused in future while in care.

I never asked for any of it.

CHAPTER 11

AFTERWORD

In writing *"Knocking on the Wall"*, a project which took years in the making, I have tried to illustrate how abuse in care impacts on many areas of my life.

It has been tedious at times, and awkward, because it is difficult to be 100% accurate in recollecting often painful memories as well as hard work in trying to put together bits of a story that actually spans more than 50 years.

In attempting to corroborate evidence and a paper trail of information relating to my time in various children's homes I found that records of my time in 2 of these homes had been destroyed by floods.

It was also very difficult to establish who or what authority might have been responsible for overseeing the home at Lagarie House, Rhu, where my brother, sister, and I were placed.

Nonetheless, I encourage everyone with similar experiences to persevere if they undertake to write their story, which at least permits the individual to start the journey to recognise and work through their own personal difficulties.

I salute all those individuals who have already written and published work about their own experiences and all those who have connected positively to the vital work of child protection.

When I started writing this book, I was trying to expel thoughts and emotions that had been buried within me for decades before I could examine them or decide what to do with them.

It is helpful to write your thoughts and feelings onto paper, keep them and look at what you wrote days or months later to allow you to review how you feel in the present or if you have learned anything useful from getting your feelings out in the open, rather than just feeling frustrated or getting angry which only feeds on itself. During the writing, which has taken over two years to date, I realised that childhood experience and the living legacy that all people carry have many threads that reach into all areas of your life.

There is no easy answer to resolving a life that was tainted by abuse, yet when you acutely feel that your life was, or is, somehow blighted, you have to try to stop getting angry or hurt about it - because when you do, it is usually the wrong people you vent your anger on. For years, I have shouted at people who did not directly have anything to do with the cruelty I suffered, but, you see, misery loves company, and that is why people who have been abused project their frustration and emotion onto anyone they cross swords with.

Childhood experiences shaped my whole life, and I know the unfair rows I had with innocent people caused many of them to walk out of my life. That was never my intention; it resulted from my lack of awareness that my problems were not their fault. I owe a lot of people an apology for the blunt and often threatening way I spoke to them, and I offer my deep apology to all those I have hurt in any way.

PART 2

KNOCKING DOWN THE WALL

CHAPTER 1
A NARRATIVE FROM NOW

Imagine your entire life as a process of crafting a persona that you gradually come to believe is your true self. Like an actor deeply immersed in their role, you begin to forget that you're acting and start taking your role seriously, forgetting that it's all make-believe. In time, the original 'you' becomes a distant memory, no longer reflective of how you live in the present.

This is precisely what happens when a child experiences abuse in any of its myriad forms. The child yearns to forget or ignore the ugliness of abuse and tries to create an alternate reality, a safe haven to escape to. This altered reality and alternative 'you' is an attempt to avoid facing the ugly truths inflicted upon the individual by their abusers. Over time, the child fantasises about a happier life or circumstances free from their experiences – but it always resurfaces, triggered by what they think, see, and hear, even long after the abuse has ended. This legacy of reaction continues to play itself out when triggered by any intrusion into the experienced person's life. The tone of voice from another person can set off an emotional response, which can manifest as anger, violence, helplessness, or avoidance of others (even those in no way connected to the individual's personal experience of abuse). This reaction is familiar to all who have experienced abuse in their lives.

It takes a long time to recognise your own 'walls' that are at the centre of your Being, and until these 'walls' are uprooted and somehow resolved, they will emerge when reactivated by that individual's internal triggers. Writing about your experience and talking through it with those who empathise with your life and experience can be incredibly helpful. Many who have experienced care or abuse cannot, or will not, explore their own suffering and, as a result, live in the past their whole lives.

I know people who are in exactly this situation and who will immediately resist any attempt to talk with them about their personal experience.

When any person finds themselves in a situation they perceive as dangerous or harmful, it results in a fight or flight reaction within their mind. No child or person deserves abuse, and when they live trying to ignore or forget it, it is often out of the mistaken belief that they are the cause of it. That is never true. I suggest it originates from abusers telling their targets that they asked for it, particularly AFTER the abuse takes place. It is an effort to shut the child off from what they feel and what that feeling might make them do – like going and reporting the abuser to another person. Abusers KNOW they are contravening the law and that the child's human right to live WITHOUT abuse has been breached. Abusers will use threats if they think they are in danger of exposure for their criminal actions towards any child.

CHAPTER 2
FIGHTING YOURSELF

Part of the legacy of abuse in people's lives is low self-esteem. The idea that *you* are unworthy of happiness or success in life expresses itself in inner conflict and putting yourself down in diverse ways. For example, you might tell yourself you will never achieve that job or that qualification and that your life is worthless. These are common experiences in the life of any who suffered abuse.

Living with trauma is like having something that now and then growls in the core of your being, and at other times, it is quiet – like a wild dog, which is often almost asleep but roused very quickly when triggers occur. All abused people have their own 'triggers', but they often share common hurts, anger, or self-loathing.

That way of experiencing life is known as *fighting yourself*, or at times, in full-blown war with yourself. It is like a tiger running away from its own tail on fire. The survivor is trying to free themself of something they are constantly dragging around with them - and which is comprised of all and any incidents of abuse that they experienced as a child.

I have known times when I had put off buying a jacket or piece of clothing because I felt I was not worthy of owning it. This putting down simple wants is directly linked to my experience of abuse as a child when I was often told I would never amount to anything. It carries over even into ordinary choices one makes and, of course, is the result of prior abuse.

Repeating ritualistic patterns is another manifestation of abuse, and it can take many forms. For example, washing your hands over and over again, checking that you have locked the door when you leave the house many times, or even avoiding walking on lines when you are outdoors. All these patterns go directly to your inner quest for certainty in your life, caused by the abuse experienced decades before and which are part of any individual's experience of abuse, repeating itself even long after the abuse occurred.

CHAPTER 3
FACING THE PAST

Reacting negatively to one's past, or trying to blot it out entirely, is common to all who experienced abuse in childhood and is indeed common also for those who are targeted by sexual predators, even as older people. No person deserves to be 'used' by anyone else, and when they are, the victim has to learn to deal with the personal stamp that their ordeal will put upon their whole life.

A woman who is sexually abused will feel very similar to anyone else who has that experience. From my enquiries in writing this narrative, I have encountered many women online who have been the target of predatory men who show no regard at all for those they assault, nor any awareness or empathy for the suffering they cause in another person's life. For many women, trying to find support is a tedious and painful experience and adds to their suffering.

One lady I talked with was sexually abused by her superior at her workplace. He was a long-serving senior employee, and her battle to be heard and BELIEVED took over 2 years. Eventually, she and her family got a measure of justice through the courts, but to this day, her trauma still impacts how she feels and how she acts around men she does not know or trust.

Children with experience who cannot articulate their words or feelings can, and do, withdraw into themselves or act aggressively toward other people in an effort to exorcise the anger and hurt that has been instilled into their lives by their experience. To face up to your past is no easy thing because, after years in denial or attempts to blank it out, it is like revisiting a very deep wound that one imagines would somehow heal itself if left alone.

CHAPTER 4
RECONSTRUCTING THE PAST

In my attempts to discover my own path through the fog that resulted from years of abuse meted out when I was in Children's Homes, I have realised that it is impossible to bury the past. One's experience is part of the fabric of one's life and to try to deny it is futile. Anything one represses will express itself in other ways.

You could relate this to denying you have a toothache. Eventually, if the pain is not addressed, it will compel you to visit the dentist. So, too, it is with repressed suffering, and I have experienced many examples of this in my life, from my teenage years until now.

Pain, whether it is physical or psychological, demands an answer. Now, some might try to mask their pain with drugs or drink, but ultimately, they come full circle and feel like they are actually right back where they started from. Therefore, I can only say to readers that if you have Core Experience Unresolved issues in your life, then your way forward is firstly to acknowledge these and start looking at how to resolve them.

It is not easy to jump in because this kind of experience is embarrassing, and it is very common among Care-Experienced people who are often personally reluctant to look into experiences that were an affront to their dignity and very existence.

It requires self-honesty and friendly support from people who are experienced in addressing these very raw areas of our lives. I had a lot of support in writing my first book, 'Knocking On The Wall,' and without that support, it is very unlikely I would have written that book. The process of deconstructing the past necessitates a journey in time, back to when the abuse happened. It requires an evaluation of the actual experience and then the acceptance that I did NOT deserve what took place.

It is not so much that one was in 'the wrong place at the wrong time,' it is, in fact, that one was in a situation where those in authority 'abused' their position of trust. One could draw up a list of separate incidents, compile a dossier of a kind and try to work out each specific 'experience', and load pages with graphic content. Yet even as I have done just that in my head, that in itself, does not remove the years of impact that I have gone through.

If you drew a graph about each incident, it would look something like this:

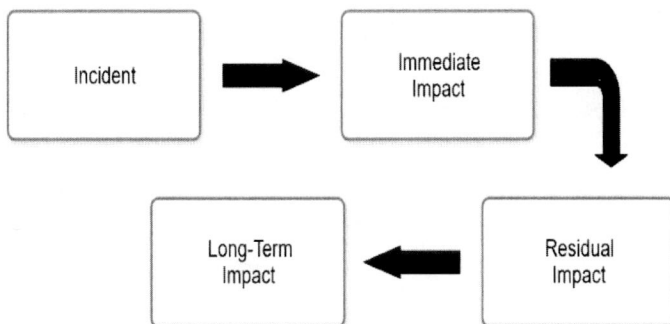

This would naturally include suffering/pain, anxiety, anger, outrage, regret, self-hate, and the desire for justice.

Each of these factors are painful in themselves, and can repeat throughout the years, whenever any circumstance arises that reminds one of any, or all, of these very real memories.

CHAPTER 5

LIVING IN THE NOW

Over the past few years, from 2016 until now, I have tried to work through issues that are part of the fabric of my life. This arises from my recognition that the 'walls' within my life have, for many years, impeded me and stopped me from trusting people or situations in life. This has also manifested in a self-distrust and in living *reactively* rather than *pro-actively.*

You could say I have been, in my own way, blocking myself from moving forward progressively or positively. For example, I find it difficult at times to take decisions, because my lack of trust in myself and other people. I have often applied for jobs that I have no ability to do, then worried that I might actually get the job.

I have reasoned that, subconsciously, I have been trying to prove to myself that I am worthy of a job that pays more or has greater prospects. I can say that I think this is part of the impact of the abuse I suffered when I was very young. Low self-esteem is real in my life.

The opposite of 'aiming too high' is 'aiming too low', and I have done physical menial jobs that most folk would merit as 'deep-body work', because in my way of thinking, that was all I deserved.

To evolve past one's experience of abuse and its impact, requires self-examination and learning to accept what you are actually good at, be it academic or practical. Furthermore, one has to realise that self-denigration is linked to the experience of abuse which often teaches the victim that they were 'worthless'.

Years of thinking that you deserve nothing evolves into an outlook that is negative. It is never deserved by anyone who is care-experienced. It is, in truth, unwanted baggage from the past.

CHAPTER 6

TIME DOES NOT REVERSE

What any individual *DOES, THINKS, OR SAYS* cannot be undone. ACTION, THOUGHT, and WORDS once expressed, are part of you forever – even if you try to ignore or forget them.

Those with negative care experiences know this all too well and live with the legacy of that. For every action, there is a reaction. For every thought and word one has and says, so too do these bear fruit, like planting a seed that grows into its mature form.

Child abuse of any kind will lead the individual who experienced it into a life of suffering and this manifests in many ways, both subtle and apparent. The mind of a child is naturally trusting when very young and also very retentive and like a tape recorder. Their mind's 'record' whatever is said and stores it in the subconscious as well as the conscious mind, to replay whenever the child experiences any situation or experience. It 're-triggers' the memories of good or bad experiences.

This is common in all who experience abuse of any kind, and from my experience of talking with many other people who have similar experience to me, I know that all of us share emotions and thoughts and an outlook that is linked by suffering.

No-one can UNDO their past. Instead they have to learn to live with the reality of the suffering experienced. This may take up most of the individual's time, especially if the individual has lived in a state of long-term denial and has used other means to try to close off painful memories from their life.

That is why one often encounters people who are alcoholics or addicted to drugs among the community of those who have negative care experiences or experienced abuse at any stage of their lives. A person may house an addiction treated by a doctor, where the patient got involved in drugs as a means of blotting out painful memories from their childhood. And if that person is not treated holistically - ie as a whole person whose past is disclosed - the likely outcome may be a temporary fix with the individual returning to the world of dependency for relief.

I have known people who are addicts, or substance-reliant, who have temporarily got off drugs only to return to them when they felt under threat - from either their own emotions or from how other people relate with them. You could say that some of those using drugs regard their use as a sort of protective shield from the world or from 'outside influences'.

The most positive approach to helping drug users trying to find a way to stop using is one that deals with the person NOT as an addict, but as a person caught in a cycle, wherein, the repeated use of drugs is 'fuelled' by their 'inner life' - ie how they see the world and the people in it.

Everyone, regardless of where they are in the world, has their own set of 'triggers' or dislikes, stemming from painful experiences. These may not always be as profound or challenging to overcome as the memories and pain of abuse, but they are significant, nonetheless.

The truth is, everyone has their own life journey, and it's uncommon to encounter someone who can claim they carry no emotional baggage from their past. In fact, I am yet to come across such a person.

CHAPTER 7

INTO THE VORTEX

In the care-experienced community, there is a shared understanding that our histories intertwine with those of others we meet on our journey - making sense of our lives and our memories. As I listen and relate my own experiences, I realise the striking similarities in the lives of those who have been similarly affected. By connecting with others who have parallel histories, individuals can start to move beyond their internal barriers, recognising that we are not alone and that others have also walked this challenging path. While this doesn't necessarily make the journey easier, it offers comfort in knowing there's shared understanding and relatability, especially regarding feelings that might seem clumsy or awkward.

Finding links with other people who share similar histories and common ground, an individual may find they are able to progress beyond their own inner walls, realising that other people have walked that very same road. This does not mean that it is any easier, but it does mean that one is *NOT alone* and that other people can relate to experience which causes negative inward feelings. The truth is, though, that barriers CAN be overcome and that care experienced people *CAN* gradually reach a point where their painful memories are lessened and their burden reduced.

Readers may know from personal experience the 'residual suffering', but even if they do not, they will at least know that working through negative emotions is the right way to proceed. It is very useful to empathise with anyone you meet and be open to learning where their experience has taken them— especially if you are working in a supporting role.

Your empathy will be recognised by those with whom you are working, and that creates a bridge or a pathway for you to learn more and be regarded as trustworthy by people who have known and experienced a betrayal of trust at any level.

CHAPTER 8

DANGEROUS SECRETS

'Live openly and keep no secrets.' (TS)

I knew many other people in my youth who had experienced abuse of all sorts, at home, at school, among their peers and in Children's Homes or Care. Some of them are no longer alive, and it was, in my opinion, the secrecy that took their lives.

At 16, one boy I knew from Ponton House Lads' Residence hanged himself because he could not disclose his abuse to anyone else.

The world is full of secrets and it is my view that many of those are dangerous and cause suffering.

The deep shame and embarrassment of abuse leads the individual into a life that puts a wall around them to keep out other people, and also because many of them were abused by predators who used open and subliminal threats against the individual to conceal what they were doing.

This experience matures over the years into an unwillingness either to talk about or disclose the abuse. I cannot emphasise enough how damaging this is for people, who can go on for years or for life, living in an enclosed personal world fraught with worry that their innermost 'secrets' should be revealed and exposed to the world.

It does not matter that they were innocent of any crime, or that they were targeted by predators. For the individual concerned, they live worrying about exposure.

Readers might think that it is logical or easy to disclose all to some other person. It is not. To get to a point where one could feel relaxed and comfortable to 'open up' does *NOT* arrive in the lives of *all* abused people. Many victims *NEVER* talk about their experiences and die, taking all their suffering to the grave. Those who NEVER disclose have not really lived and have had all or most of their lives stolen from them and never returned.

I think my stepfather had many secrets. He drank far more than was good for him, and drink had the effect of setting him alight and sensitive to any noise. A neighbour walking across the floor in the flat above would set him into a rage, which would quickly turn into abuse, verbally and physically, towards my mother, brother, sister, or me - if any of us were in the vicinity.

I often think he was abused when he was a child because, when he drank, his anger and violence at times far surpassed any actual event. Even if it was just that you made a noise.

He would listen to Wagner's Valkyrie or Götterdämmerung with the volume very loud and never seem to react violently to that; yet if any of the family closed a door noisily, he would talk angrily at volume and follow it up with belting the offender. He was smart enough to show respect to law officers or grown men, as I witnessed more than once. His anger and violence were reserved for my mother and her children. There is little question that he was a troubled man.

DANGEROUS SECRETS

All of my writing and thinking have shown me that secrecy and the hiding of secrets have a negative effect on anyone caught in that maze of deceit, towards self or other people.

When long-kept secrets are exposed, they result in suffering, especially if they are related to abuse. Predators and those who cover up or hide abuse are storing up secrets which one day must come out, and the fact that there have been 'official' cover-ups only adds to the suffering of those who were targeted. It is shameful that many abused people were not believed or had nowhere to turn to and were compelled to live in suffering for most of, or all of, their lives. That is inexcusable in my view.

CHAPTER 9

FACING THE FUTURE

The 'Future' is connected to the present, just as the present is connected with the past. Everyone in the world has a past and present, and all look at the FUTURE as if it is separated. However, you could say that there is really only THIS MOMENT, here and now, where you are reading these words by which I am trying to illustrate how everything in one's life is connected with everything else.

For care-experienced people, the seemingly solid illusions of life are often puzzling, because abuse upsets the equilibrium in the lives of those who experience it. As most people grow older, they become creatures of habit. They do everyday things in almost ritualistic ways. They may wear particular clothing on a Monday or like tea at 4 o'clock every day, yet *if* they were abused when they were young, then their 'socialisation' patterns are disrupted, which can lead to a *reactive* rather than *proactive* outlook in life.

When I was at school in the 1950s and 60s, I had already experienced abuse, and I know that impacted my ability and willingness to learn and absorb what I was being taught in school. 'Problem Children' were in most schools, and I recall that there were extra classes for what they called 'slow learners'.

I can only speculate how many of the children who attended these classes were abused children who had never told anyone about it. This could explain too why many children were 'disruptive' in class. Without knowing particular details of 'difficult' children, it is almost impossible for teachers to understand the reasons why not all children act in the same way or can conform to the routines that are common practice in school, given that children go to school to learn, to socialise, as well as do 'lessons'. Care-experienced children have more to overcome to enable them to learn and develop. In turn help them to 'face the future' with confidence.

My own schooling was not easy, and I often found myself *NOT* wanting to be there at all. Even in primary school, with the 'strap' and 'bullying' and 'school fights', the experience of being in a learning process was not ideal. There were no support systems in these times and for those of my generation, school was rather a rite of passage, rather than instruction for a productive or meaningful future.

CHAPTER 10

GETTING TO KNOW ME

The age-old question common to all who try to figure out what life is about or what they are about is expressed in the question,, *'Who Am I?'*

For most of us, life is 'about' getting ahead, finding our niche in the world, and acquiring the means to live without want. Living a full, happy, and fulfilled life is a 'goal' that most people set themselves and which society encourages through schooling, influence, and television advertising.

The idea of having 'more' equates to happiness everywhere. I point out this anomaly to illustrate how 'double-speak' expresses itself because, on far too many occasions, I was told one thing by one person and something altogether different by another. This was constant within the homes I was placed in, and it was very difficult trying to heed 'advice' from one, *knowing* that to do so meant stepping on someone else's toes.

At age 16, I had no idea which way to go, and this, too, is directly linked to what I had experienced in the hurly-burly of Children's Homes. Over the years, one learned that to see through all the barriers would take effort and willingness to look at the past in all its rawness and difficulty.

In writing about my life and my experience, I have learned a little about what makes me the person I am, and I see I have yet to learn more. My stepfather used to say, 'Learning is Permanent', and while my experiences at his hands were not positive, he was accurate on that point. No one is ever too old to learn something new. You could say learning about yourself never ends.

For most people, the term 'Work in Progress' would seem most appropriate since the art of living is just like painting a portrait and adding to it along the way. To know one's LIMITS to any degree begins loosening the inner chains common to all with Care Experience.

CHAPTER 11
CONCLUSION

How many words does one have to write until all the inner shit is exorcised? In fact, there is no answer to that question, as individually all those impacted by child abuse must walk their own path of resolution.

My own life impacted for decades has been a rollercoaster of emotion. I had many years of trying to understand the mess that comprised 'myself' with all the residual hurt, anger and outrage. Now, I see I have learned something about working with my inner emotion, yet, knowing there is more *TO* learn.

Unravelling past conflict is akin to investigating crime. One has to look at all the elements and evidence to try to formulate a presentable argument and analysis that will hold water and convince others of the truth and accuracy of your life story. Convincing yourself is *ALSO* a very important part of this process.

Anyone who has done this knows it is extremely difficult and that you are against many who oppose your probing the uncomfortable truths of past abuse.

Nonetheless, it has to go on until it is ended through the full realisation that one no longer *HAS* to CARRY THE BAGGAGE from a disrupted childhood.

I was with my brother and sister at the Children's Home at Rhu, where I first learned that child abuse is very real and it was the way of life in that place for and toward anyone who got in the way of the Matron. As far as I know, children who went there had to be from families with a sea-going working person in the Merchant Navy or on deep-sea vessels.

Children at home or in care who live under the threat of violence or abuse will naturally try to find ways to survive in hostile environments. That is a fact. It also carries over into their later years in ways that are not easy to either talk about or ever forget.

No one has any right to abuse or violate children, and this story has led me into areas that, for over 50 years, I refused to acknowledge.

In writing "Knocking on the Wall" and "Knocking Down the Wall", I have tried to explain as best as I can what the impact is like in later years. It is not a great work nor does it give as much insight as some other writers could, but it is an accurate record of my experience of the CARE System.

If just one reader finds my account of some help, it will have served the purpose (or one of them at least) for which it was written.

At 6 years old, I had already known the terror of being beaten and intimidated in care while I was in the children's home in Rhu. I was used and abused in all three care homes between the ages of 6 to 16. I was subjected to sexual, physical and emotional abuse to the degree that I have never forgotten it or the impact it has had (and is still having) on my life. I am now 73 years of age, and I can look back at what the *"Care and Protection"* experience meant (and means) in my life.

CONCLUSION

It was an assault and invasion on my person, and it left scars that influenced me and caused me to deeply distrust those in authority and to resent the power given to them by Local Central Authorities. It also showed me that the misuse/abuse of public trust is criminal, and those who abuse others in their care are the lowest form of human life in the world.

POETRY

(These poems were written over years and are all related to my view of life and the changing inner world that is myself).

DEPERSONALISATION

First they took his freedom
Then they took his clothes
Then they gave him an identity tag
Then they cut his hair
Then they told him what to do
And when to do it
Then they told him when to eat
And when to sleep
And when to awaken

They told him when he could
Go out and when to return
Then they told him
It was for his own good
This was all done

In the name of "Welfare"
Like sour fruit
It left a taste in his mouth
That still remains.

SMALL THINKING MAN

Walking without eyes
He doesn't see the world
Except through previously learned lies
Told him when young
Put him in chains
Stopped him from growing
Filled him with pain. Years further on
He questions everything He wants to awaken
He just wants to sing.
He saw a teacher
Travelling like in flight
He listened, he questioned
'Til he saw the light
Thereafter his duty
To do what he can
To awaken what truly is
His fellow man

PRISON BARS

It is not bars a prison makes
It is what is in your head.
For each constructs within the mind
Their walls and locks and chains.
If you can look just for a while
At the views that you believe
You will start to see it is yourself
Whom you yourself deceive.
Freedom in the true sense
Is the end of all self-illusion.
Walk in love – harm no one.

ENTRY THE FIRST

Look around the world and see
The ways of this humanity
The illusion that we all believe
The means and methods we conceive.
Look for ways to unite the world
Expose the falsehoods and the lie
See the futility of pain and war
There's none are perfect, yet we can try.
Look at what you say you believe
Is it worth causing others pain?
When the illusion finally goes
Then you see what can remain.
Look at how you can be of use
To the others and your own
None are outwith your circle of friends
Even if the lie has grown

MY SON LEO

My son Leo is a fine tall lad
He is kind and intelligent too
He's a guy more professional than his dad.
Do I love him?
Sure I do!
He works hard and is straightforward
And has good looks
And a heart that is open and tender
He thinks well of all of those
Whom he meets in the world
And his help he would willingly tender.
I am proud of my son
Though I don't tell him so
But when he reads this ode
I trust he will know.
Leo, may you achieve your heart's wish

HOW IT IS

Like waves at the seaside
Memories overflow and ebb
Things past still have significance
And visit when they like.
Young people who suffer
Later find their voice articulating
To some degree
Their life experience.
When young people are raised in love
Happiness follows.

LISTEN

When it is dark
The sun is shining
When it is light
The sun is shining
– Always.

ALAN WATTS ODE
(AUTHOR OF THE SUPREME IDENTITY)

If I could live my life again
I would change so much of it
I would try to find an open way
And not just fail or quit.
I'd like to see the end of war
And peace in every land
No hunger, nor no poverty
And all lending a hand.
Life is a journey, that's for sure
With open doors and walls
An ever revealing ageless tale
As ever I recall.
Here is a wish that everyone
Will find their own unique path
And at the last when all is done
They'll have a long hearty laugh.

SUNRISE?

When I was young I knew
That you didn't care
I was just another child alone
I wasn't really there
Like I was unseen, unheard
I had no voice, no choice
I wasn't a human person I had no right
No say in what I did or
Where I went
Told and controlled without knowing why
The only thing real
Was the pain I feel
From realising that the word
"Care" is considered nothing
Without applying genuine love
When working with those to whom
Love is a stranger.

LOOKING IN FROM THE OUTSIDE

See the people laughing
Feeling, as they do, connected
To their world, their lives –
Yet- Looking from the outside
Knowing that you are not invited
Like the story of Oliver Twist
The boy who asked for more
And was met with cruel indifference and anger
Who was passed from pillar
To post - before he finally
Knew any real happiness.
Children who are abused
Know of what is written here
They require no intellectual
Explanation, - they require
Human love. <u>That Is All</u>

GO FORWARD WITH LOVE

Know this:- you were <u>not</u>
(nor are you now) to <u>blame</u>
You did not <u>deserve</u> to
Suffer the cruelty or ulterior
Motives of other people
You are no less a person for
Having been abused
You are not dirty or inferior
For being abused by others
You have the right to look for happiness
You have the right to succeed
You have the right to love and be loved
You are NOT to blame
Go forward, knowing that the experience you have
Is known by other people.
Try to find happiness

THE GLASS IS NOT HALF EMPTY,
THE GLASS IS HALF FULL

To see the good in everything
You only need to look
There's good in plants and trees as well
There's good in a good book.
The smile upon an infant's face
The twinkle in an old man's eye
The light that shines on all who dwell
From the sun high in the sky.
There's good in animals
And even those whom you don't like
May one day be your pals.
There's good in travel, good in art
And good in films and songs
If more folk looked toward that good
There'd surely be less wrongs.
The moral of this little verse
Is very plain to see
Cheer up and try to do your best
For all Humanity.

TO YOU (TO EVERY PERSON)

Here is my word to you
I begin from where I am
Which is always here, right here,
No other place can I live.
I apologise to you
For my errors and my pride
I need to be far nicer
I must learn to abide.
May your path be warm and happy
May your heart be ever pure
May you find the life you truly want
This is my wish for you.

AWAKEN AS SOON AS LIFE ALLOWS

From one trap to another
As the flower of life experience unfolds
I try to see through these illusions
It might take more time Than this one life
To finally, no longer, Have to recall the past
When at once I want to say

A LESSON TO BE LEARNED

Whatever you do, just do what you can
No one's perfect, when the shit hits the fan
You can only try, you can only smile
And believe that the effort is worthwhile.
Don't worry if you get it wrong
Just keep on trying as you go along
Everyone else is the same as you
As time goes on, you'll see that's true.

THE NIGHT I RAN AWAY

It was around 8 PM, I was alone
My mother and stepfather were both at home.
He was drinking, I made a sound
Next thing I knew, I was on the ground.

Shouting and swearing, filled the room
He had on his boots, I saw in the gloom.
He was kicking and slapping, I rolled on the floor,
I covered my face, then saw a door.

He dragged me up, onto my feet
I had on no shoes, I was feeling the heat.
Dressed only in trousers with no shirt nor top,
I silently wished for the violence to stop.

He paused, for a second, well out of buff,
I knew in that instant, that I had enough.
I tore through the front door
and fled down the stair
He roared and he threatened,
but I didn't care.

I ran all the way to the house of a friend,
I was bloodied and battered
my tears would not end.
I was taken inside and my bruises were sore

I cried out what happened,
couldn't take this no more.

I never returned to my family home,
I stayed with an aunt, in the world on my own.
I passed into Care and continued in school
My sole Graduation
of Life as a Fool.

ON BEING MISUNDERSTOOD

Caution is the operative word
If one wishes to be heard
And not have one's speech soundly blurred
Or have one's meaning quickly slurred
By people with whom one converses
While sitting quietly on our 'erses
And eating cakes and drinking tea
This makes for pleasing company.

A word or two quietly said
With care and taste will reach the head
The brainbox of the other party
So mind and say naught that is clarty,
Especially when engaged in drink
For that can alter the way we think
And drinking, that which doth ferment
Can quickly lead to argument.

In conclusion may I say
That silence is the proper way
To pass the message properly
The less you speak, the more you say.

KYE – HO!

Through all these lands
Let the true warrior spirit arise!
The warriorship that defeats
Delusion, ignorance and aggression
Mankind's true 'enemies'
Externalised as 'other' in our ignorance
May the teaching of Milarepa the Renunciate
Open the Eye of Wisdom
In all beings.

The sun arose at midnight
The Doors of Perception were cleansed
And the scheme of things
Seen clearly
For the first time.

*(Kye – Ho is a Tibetan expression meaning
'Awake' or 'Attention')*

REFLECTION

Within the walls of memory
The shadows of the past
I walk outside, looking out,
The world is changing fast
From early years, 'til present day
The reactive painful view
That lingers on, like frozen rain
Touching all that I must do
Communicating what it is
No easy task I see
For each must walk in their own shoes
Until they can be free
The words on paper can't transmit
Except in clumsy way
What one wants to articulate
To melt the past away.

THE QUEST FOR INNOCENCE

Where have you brought me to life?
What is this place?
By god, I've read the history books, a catalogue of despair,
death, and suffering.
Why do we exist?
Where are we and where are we going?
Do we live merely to die?
To wander aimlessly, seeking pleasure
And avoiding pain, wherever we may find it?
There are those who wallow in pleasure
There are those who wallow in pain
There are people spouting truths
Politicians lying through their teeth.

What is this, this existence, which marks everyone
Who is born into this plane of existence?
I must come back to myself
for some kind of reference
For I trust no one.
I love
My love is fragmented
Emotions crash and thunder within our flesh form
Mind is full of wonder, puzzlement, question, doubt
Sometimes content to just observe.

To look without naming what we see
And to see what exists, without language
Without labels attaching themselves
To see the world with innocent eyes!

CLARION CALL

Society listen
You educate our people
Exercise social control
Then you tell us that animals
Ain't got no soul
There ain't no sense in you
Yet you claim to be right
You're so mixed up
You ain't never seen the light
Your armies and your navies
And your air force too
Will be of little use
When Brother Death calls on you
You think death is an enemy
But death is a friend
You'll see Death in the beginning
'cause Death ain't the end.

ABOUT THE AUTHOR

Trevor Swistchew has worked on writing for over 40 years. He has published poetry in many formats and is a songwriter and guitar player recording original songs relating to his experiences in Children's Homes, which has impacted his life for more than five decades.

He has posted over 25k tweets online and campaigned on issues he is close to. He is now a full-time writer and human rights campaigner.

Anyone working to protect children from predators can access his work by email.

Link with Trevor at:
t.swistchew65@gmail.com

If you liked this book, please leave a review on Amazon or Goodreads. Also, if you want to express any view on this work, you may email Trevor at the address above. Thank You for reading this work.

If you know someone who works to protect children in any capacity – you can email him at the email address above for a free copy of his earlier work.

ACKNOWLEDGEMENTS

If YOU were abused, I encourage you to think about your experience, write your story down and take it to the National Enquiry (contact details can be found online).

What happened to you WILL happen to others also - that is why your input is vital to help the prevention of abuse toward other children in future.

I want to record a huge Thank You to the following;

Elizabeth, my partner, for typing out most of the work and correcting words and grammar as required. As well as for all her efforts at the early stages and typing out a lot of my earlier work.

Future Pathways (Sophie Jenkins), who listened to my reading chapters of the first book of my work and encouraged me to finish the first manuscript. Also to John Crawford for encouraging my writing.

My editor, Mary Turner Thomson, from The Book Whisperers, for guidance and good advice on continuing and supporting in creating this combined book. I am hugely grateful for all the support from The Book Whisperers, including cover design, editing, publishing and marketing support.

Warren McKean, my fellow guitar-playing friend who told me to keep writing.

There are far too many other people to list, who encouraged me in writing this book and organisations who were positive and offered advice, many of whom are supportive to anyone who was abused in their youth.

If this book inspires you to write your own story, then it has achieved its purpose. I sincerely hope it helps others articulate and share their experiences, finding healing through that process.